What if we do NOThing?

NUCLEAR PROLIFERATION

Joseph Harris

FRANKLIN WATTS
LONDON•SYDNEY

First published in 2009 by Franklin Watts

Copyright © 2009 Arcturus Publishing Limited

Franklin Watts
338 Euston Road
London NW1 3BH

Franklin Watts Australia
Level 17/207 Kent Street, Sydney, NSW 2000

Produced by Arcturus Publishing Limited,
26/27 Bickels Yard, 151-153 Bermondsey Street,
London SE1 3HA

Series concept: Alex Woolf
Editor: Alex Woolf
Designer: Phipps Design
Picture researcher: Alex Woolf

A CIP catalogue record for this book is available
from the British Library.

Dewey Decimal Classification Number: 333.792' 4

ISBN 978 0 7496 8749 6

Printed in China

Franklin Watts is a division of Hachette Children's
Books, an Hachette UK company.
www.hachette.co.uk

Picture Credits
Corbis: cover *top right* (Dallas and John Heaton/Free Agents
Limited), 10 (Bettmann), 14 (Jean-Paul Pelissier/Reuters), 16
(Bettmann), 19 (Abedin Taherkenareh/epa), 20 (Pakistan Military
Department/Handout/Reuters), 31 (Bettmann), 33 (Neville
Elder/Corbis Sygma), 35 (Reuters), 36 (Reuters), 38 (Reuters),
cover *bottom left* and 41 (Reuters), 44 (Kimmasa Mayama/epa).
Getty Images: 8 (George Silk/Time & Life Pictures), 26 (Scott
Peterson), 28 (Arif Ali/AFP), 43 (Digital Globe).
PA Photos: 24 (Dennis Cook/AP).
Rex Features: 13 (Everett Collection).
Science Photo Library: cover *background* and 4 (US Department of
Energy), 7 (Roger Harris), 23 (US Department of Energy).

Cover pictures
bottom left: A South Korean protester burns North Korea's
national flag beside mock nuclear missiles during an anti-North
Korea protest in Seoul, South Korea, on 15 August 2003.
top right: The Atomic Bomb Memorial Dome in Hiroshima, Japan.
background: The mushroom cloud produced by the detonation of a
15-kiloton nuclear bomb. The test was carried out by the United
States in Nevada on 25 May 1953.

Every attempt has been made to clear copyright. Should there be
any inadvertent omission, please apply to the publisher for
rectification.

Contents

CHAPTER 1

The Power of Atoms

It is 2025 and Min-sik is a very worried young man. The dictator of a neighbouring state possesses nuclear weapons and is threatening to attack the South-East Asian country where Min-sik lives. The dictator has issued many such threats since he acquired nuclear weapons, but fear of retaliation by other nuclear-armed countries normally stops him from carrying them out. However, the dictator is erratic and there is no guarantee that he will be dissuaded this time. Min-sik has read books about the devastating effects of nuclear weapons. He knows that many thousands of people will die in a nuclear blast and that the radioactive fallout from the explosion will pollute the environment over a wide area. He wishes he could be free of the constant fear of nuclear attack.

Nuclear weapons are the most devastating weapons ever invented. A nuclear device produces a detonation far more powerful than any other kind of explosive. Because of their awesome power, people often refer to nuclear weapons simply as 'the Bomb'. As well as possessing enormous destructive force, nuclear weapons also leave behind harmful radioactive dust called fallout.

A nuclear explosion flings large amounts of hot gas, dust and debris into the air above a test site in Nevada, USA. The result is an amazing shape in the sky, usually described as a mushroom cloud. The mushroom cloud became the symbol of the nuclear age and the threat of a terribly destructive war. Many people had nightmares in which these menacing mushroom clouds loomed over their countries.

THE POWER OF BOMBS

This chart shows the estimated numbers killed in some bomb attacks on civilian targets during World War II, and the tonnage of bombs used. The incredible power of the nuclear weapons, compared with other types of bombs, is clear.

Date	City	Type of bombs	Tonnage of bombs	Numbers killed
7 September 1940 to 11 May 1941	London and other UK cities (the Blitz)	Explosives and incendiaries	18,000	40,000-43,000
30 May 1942	Cologne	Explosives and incendiaries	1,455	450-500
28 July 1943	Hamburg	Explosives and incendiaries	2,313	30,000-40,000
14-15 February 1945	Dresden	Explosives and incendiaries	2,660	30,000-35,000
6 August 1945	Hiroshima	Nuclear (uranium)	4	90,000-140,000
9 August 1945	Nagasaki	Nuclear (plutonium)	4.5	60,000-80,000

Sources: www.historyplace.com/worldwar2/timeline/about-blitz.htm; Royal Air Force - www.raf.mod.uk/bombercommand/thousands.html; Air Force Historical Studies Office - www.airforcehistory.hq.af.mil/PopTopics/dresden.htm; www.historylearningsite.co.uk/hamburg_bombing_1943.htm; Radiation Effects Research Foundation: www.rerf.or.jp/general/qa_e/qa1.html

One nuclear explosion can destroy a city. A large number could ruin the earth's environment and climate, producing a nuclear winter in which the planet would cool and many species would become extinct. An all-out nuclear war could destroy human civilization and perhaps all life on earth. The impact of nuclear weapons is so horrific that no sane person wants to see them used, and many people would like them to be dismantled.

However, since the United States manufactured the first nuclear weapon in 1945, huge numbers have been produced. Today, nine countries have nuclear weapons. Between them they possess thousands. The spread of nuclear weapons to different countries is called nuclear proliferation. The more these weapons proliferate, the greater the danger of a nuclear war.

Scientific breakthrough

Twentieth-century scientific discoveries led to the creation of 'the Bomb'. The great physicist Albert Einstein showed that mass (matter or physical substance) could be transformed into energy (the driving force that makes things happen). Once this was understood, scientists began practical experiments to convert mass into energy.

Nuclear energy

In order to release energy, scientists had to split apart the building blocks of matter, which are called atoms. Scientists once believed that atoms were the smallest things in the universe, but they later discovered even smaller units, called particles. At the centre of every atom there is a cluster of particles known as its nucleus (plural: nuclei). Splitting the nucleus of an atom proved to be the key to releasing some of its mass as energy. This is how nuclear energy got its name: its power comes from the *nucleus* of an *atom*, so it is called *nuclear* or *atomic* energy. Scientists prefer the word fission to 'splitting', so *nuclear* (or *atomic*) *fission* describes the process they use to create nuclear energy.

ALBERT EINSTEIN

Einstein (1879-1955) was the most famous scientist of the 20th century. Born in Germany, he made his most important discoveries while working in the Swiss Patent Office in Bern. His Special Theory of Relativity, published in 1905, proved that matter and energy were related. A famous equation, $E = mc^2$, shows that a small mass can become a large amount of energy, since the potential energy of a mass *(E)* is calculated by multiplying the mass *(m)* by the speed of light *(c)* squared (multiplied by itself). Light travels at 299,792,458 metres per second, so the speed of light squared is an extremely high number. This is why relatively small amounts of nuclear fuel can produce enormous explosions.

Nuclear power does not have to be used solely for weapons. Nowadays nuclear power stations produce electricity that powers homes, offices and factories. However, nuclear power and nuclear weapons use similar technology. The radioactive fuel and waste used in power stations can be modified for use in weapons. This means that some countries or groups might try to use civilian nuclear power programmes as a front for developing nuclear weapons.

The Manhattan Project

In August 1939, Einstein wrote a letter to the US President, Franklin Delano Roosevelt. He suggested that it was possible to use atomic

fission to create a weapon of unprecedented power. The aggressive Nazi regime in Germany was on the march, and Einstein was worried that German scientists might master the technology first. Roosevelt ordered research to begin. Soon afterwards, World War II (1939–1945) broke out.

The work intensified after the United States entered the war in December 1941. Huge resources were poured into a new initiative, the Manhattan Project, based at Los Alamos, New Mexico. It involved thousands of people and multiple sites, and cost nearly $2 billion.

This image represents a single atom of matter. Each of the coloured spheres is a sub-atomic particle. The central cluster of green and red particles is the nucleus of the atom. The green particles are neutrons and the red ones are protons. The blue particles that circle the nucleus are electrons.

The scientists' objective was to create a fission chain reaction. This meant that when an atom was split, the particles given off would split the nuclei of other atoms, which would split still others, and so on. The chain reaction could only be achieved by using certain rare forms (or isotopes) of radioactive materials such as uranium and plutonium. Radioactive materials are materials that emit energy in the form of streams of particles. They do this because of the decay of their unstable atoms.

On 16 July 1945, after three years of research, the scientists of the Manhattan Project succeeded in creating a fission chain reaction in a mass of plutonium. A test in the desert, code-named Trinity, produced the world's first nuclear detonation. The explosion had a force equivalent to 19 kilotons (19,000 tons of TNT) and lit up the

The Japanese city of Hiroshima, devastated by the atomic bomb dropped on 6 August 1945. The nuclear shock wave flattened most of the city, leaving only a few strongly constructed buildings standing.

sky over the New Mexico test site. An enormous ball of fire shot upwards, crowned by a mushroom-shaped plume of vapour and debris. Some of the scientists, including the head of the project, J Robert Oppenheimer, were appalled by the destructive power of the new weapon they had created.

Hiroshima and Nagasaki

Soon afterwards, the United States used nuclear bombs for the first time as weapons of war. Between 1941 and 1945, the United States had been waging war against Japan in the Pacific Ocean. By 1945, the United States was on the verge of victory, but Japan refused to surrender. It seemed as though the United States would have to invade mainland Japan to end the war. Such an invasion would likely cost the lives of many thousands of soldiers and civilians. The US government decided instead to use its nuclear bombs on two Japanese cities to persuade the Japanese government to surrender.

On 6 August 1945, a nuclear bomb, code-named 'Little Boy', was dropped on the city of Hiroshima. The bomb's core was made up of uranium, and it had an explosive force of 20 kilotons. The blast instantly killed thousands. Many who survived the explosion suffered horrific injuries and died slow, painful deaths later. Two-thirds of the city was levelled, and much of the rest was set on fire. Three days later, a 22-kiloton plutonium bomb, codenamed 'Fat Man', was dropped on Nagasaki. Japan surrendered within a few days.

So far, these have been the only times nuclear weapons have been used in war. However, the destruction of the two cities provided a chilling demonstration of what nuclear weapons could do, and the proliferation of such weapons has come to be recognized as one of the great problems of the modern age.

DEBATE

You are in charge

You are a government minister attending a debate about the ethics of nuclear weapons. The topic of discussion is whether your country should keep or dispose of its nuclear weapons. What do you think?

■ We should get rid of our nuclear weapons, regardless of what other nations do. We must set an example.

■ We *might* get rid of our nuclear weapons, but only if other nations agree to do the same.

■ We should keep our nuclear weapons – we might need them to defend ourselves or to deter others from attacking us.

CHAPTER 2

The Nuclear Arms Race

It is 2025. Nina lives in a small mountain village. She spends most of her time in the fields, looking after the crops. Nina's parents tell her that life was once much easier and more pleasant, but that years earlier a nuclear war badly damaged the planet. Radioactive dust from nuclear explosions has clouded the atmosphere, making it hard for the sun's rays to get through. This has caused a catastrophic drop in temperature. Nina's country used to have warm summers and mild winters. Now the winters are so cold that nothing can be grown during them. The village faces a constant struggle to harvest enough to get through the winter. Other surviving settlements are equally poor and isolated from one another.

After World War II (1939–1945), a bitter rivalry developed between the world's two superpowers, the United States and the communist Soviet Union, or USSR (a huge state, centred on present-day Russia, that no longer exists). Many of the world's nations allied themselves to one or other of the superpowers. For example, the democracies of Western Europe backed the United States, while most of Eastern Europe became part of the communist alliance. The division of the world into two armed

Ethel and Julius Rosenberg leave the Federal Court in New York City. The Rosenbergs were tried and convicted of passing on atomic secrets to the Soviet Union. They were executed on 19 June 1953. This was the only execution of civilians for espionage during the Cold War.

camps dominated international politics for over 40 years. The period is known as the Cold War – 'cold' because the rivalry was often intensely hostile and threatening but never led to a 'hot', shooting war between the superpowers. The Cold War lasted until 1991, when the Soviet Union collapsed.

The superpower rivalry led to the first nuclear proliferation, when the Soviets successfully tested a nuclear bomb in 1949. This ended the US nuclear monopoly. People now had to live with the possibility of a war in which both sides might use nuclear weapons.

GLOBAL STOCKPILE OF NUCLEAR WEAPONS

This table shows the numbers of weapons possessed by each of the five nuclear powers during the Cold War.

	United States	Soviet Union	UK	France	China
1945	6	0	0	0	0
1950	369	5	0	0	0
1955	3,057	200	10	0	0
1960	20,434	1,605	30	0	0
1965	31,642	6,129	310	32	5
1970	26,119	11,643	280	36	75
1975	27,052	19,055	350	188	185
1980	23,764	30,062	350	250	280
1985	23,135	39,197	300	360	425
1990	21,211	33,417	300	505	430
1995	10,953	14,978*	300	500	400

* This figure refers to operational warheads possessed by Russia after the fall of the Soviet Union.

Source: Natural Resources Defense Council - www.nrdc.org/nuclear/nudb/datab19.asp

The H-bomb

The first nuclear weapons were A-bombs (short for atomic bombs). In 1952, the United States tested a new and more devastating form of nuclear weapon, the H-bomb (hydrogen bomb). It worked on a similar principle to the A-bomb, but the nuclear chain reaction took place in a different way.

The A-bombs were based on nuclear fission, in which atoms of nuclear fuel were broken apart to produce a chain reaction that releases enormous amounts of energy. The H-bomb was based on nuclear fusion. Instead of being broken apart, atoms were forced to fuse together. For this reason, H-bombs are also known as fusion bombs, or thermonuclear bombs. H-bombs produced a vast explosive yield. America's first H-bomb had a force of 7 megatons (7 million tons of TNT). It was tested on a small island in the South Pacific. Its detonation was so powerful that the island was wiped off the face of the earth.

The Soviet Union soon matched the United States' success. In 1953, it tested a 'hybrid' bomb, using elements of fusion technology. It followed this in 1955 with the detonation of a true H-bomb. Each side was now capable of deploying weapons 350 times more powerful than the bombs dropped on Hiroshima and Nagasaki.

Deterrence

Each superpower began to stockpile weapons in order to gain an advantage over the enemy – and so began a nuclear arms race. The United States had a head start, but the Soviet Union made astonishingly rapid progress.

A strategy soon evolved known as deterrence. Deterrence was based on the

THE CUBAN MISSILE CRISIS

In 1962, the nightmare of nuclear war seemed about to become a reality. The Soviet Union was secretly planning to install nuclear missiles on the territory of its ally Cuba, an island just 90 miles from the US coast. In October 1962, the Americans discovered the Soviet plan. President John F Kennedy ordered the US navy to blockade Cuba and prevent Soviet ships from delivering nuclear missiles. For a few days the world held its breath. If the Soviet ships resisted the blockade, war might well break out. Fortunately, both Kennedy and the Soviet leader, Nikita Khrushchev, realized how serious the situation was and managed to come to an agreement. The Soviet Union agreed to remove its missiles from Cuba. In return, the United States guaranteed that it would not invade the island and promised to remove its nuclear weapons from Turkey. Deterrence won the day.

idea that a nation would threaten immense retaliation if attacked, sufficient to deter (put off) an enemy from attacking.

As each superpower's arsenals grew, it soon became apparent that any nuclear exchange would mean 'mutually assured destruction' (MAD) – an attack by either side would result in the certain destruction of both. British statesman Winston Churchill famously described the situation as a 'balance of terror'.

The Cold War comes to the movies. In the 1964 comedy *Dr Strangelove*, trigger-happy General Buck Turgidson, played by George C Scott (left), tries to persuade the US president to launch a nuclear attack on the Soviet Union.

French soldiers take part in a training exercise. They are practising the procedures for dealing with a nuclear accident in which radioactive material has leaked from a nuclear weapon. They are wearing protective decontamination suits and carry equipment to scan for radiation.

By the 1960s, the United States and the Soviet Union both possessed arsenals of H-bombs. Improvements in technology meant that these could be delivered to targets around the globe via aircraft, submarines and intercontinental ballistic missiles (ICBMs) – powerful rockets that can carry nuclear warheads vast distances.

Policymakers on both sides of the Cold War divide came to believe that a nuclear war could not be won. Even a surprise attack, or first strike, would not prevent the enemy from delivering an equally devastating second strike. Radar could identify the incoming missiles and the nation under attack would be able to retaliate (strike back) before the missiles arrived. Moreover, both sides had nuclear-armed submarines and aircraft in different parts of world, ready to carry out a nuclear strike at short notice.

Cold War proliferation

The growing arsenals of the United States and the Soviet Union were not the only concern. Three other nations involved in the Cold War became independent

NUCLEAR ACCIDENTS

The arms race threatened the world with war, but it also created fears that a catastrophic accident might occur. Nuclear weapons contain conventional explosives as part of their trigger mechanisms. If these are set off accidentally, through human or mechanical error, they would probably not cause a full-scale nuclear detonation. However, harmful radioactive material from the bomb might spread over a wide area. In 1956, there was a near disaster at the Royal Air Force (RAF) base at Lakenheath in Suffolk. A B-47 bomber crashed into a storage facility containing nuclear weapons and set it on fire. Fortunately, the blaze was put out and the explosives in the nuclear weapons failed to detonate. Some experts believe that even if nuclear war is avoided, the spread of nuclear weapons will sooner or later lead to disaster.

nuclear powers – Britain in 1952, France in 1960 and China in 1964. At the time, however, the spread of nuclear weapons to other countries seemed less important than doing something about the expanding arsenals of the superpowers, which dwarfed those of their allies. Political leaders focused their energies on trying to end the superpower arms race and even to achieve some level of disarmament.

Test ban treaty

At various times, both sides in the Cold War made efforts to limit the arms race. One obvious way of doing this was to ban the testing of nuclear bombs, which polluted the atmosphere and made it easier to develop new and more powerful weapons. International talks on the subject succeeded up to a point. However, there was no way of checking with absolute certainty whether or not a country was conducting secret underground tests. So instead of an absolute ban, a Partial Test Ban Treaty was signed on 25 July 1963 that forbade tests in the earth's atmosphere, underwater and in outer space.

NUCLEAR TESTS

This chart shows the estimated number of nuclear tests by nation, carried out between 1945 and 2006

Nation	Number of tests
USA	1,030
Soviet Union/Russia	715
UK	45
France	210
China	45
India	4
Pakistan	2
North Korea	1

Source: Natural Resources Defense Council - www.nrdc.org/nuclear/nudb/datab15.asp

SALT I and II

The superpowers' arsenals grew at a fearful rate during the Cold War. Leaders on both sides recognized that this was not a good thing, but talks on disarmament always stalled. The main reason for this was that neither side trusted the other to carry out any agreed reductions. However, in 1969 the United States and the Soviet Union began serious discussions about reducing their strategic (long-range) nuclear weapons. The first round of talks, known as SALT I (Strategic Arms Limitation Treaty), produced an agreement to limit the growth of strategic arsenals. SALT I was signed in 1972. A second round of talks, known as SALT II, dragged on throughout the 1970s. It was finally signed in 1979, but was short lived. In 1986, US president Ronald Reagan withdrew from it over alleged Soviet violations.

ABM Treaty

The SALT I talks also led to the Anti-Ballistic Missile (ABM) Treaty, signed in 1972. This placed limits on the use of anti-ballistic missile systems. These are missile defence systems designed to shoot down enemy nuclear missiles. A defensive system sounds like a good thing. However, it encourages the development of new, smarter nuclear missiles, capable of penetrating the ABM shield. Furthermore, if one side believes that it is protected from the other's missiles, it might be tempted to launch a nuclear attack. These were some of the reasons

US president Ronald Reagan (left) with Soviet leader Mikhail Gorbachev. The two leaders managed to negotiate major reductions in the nuclear arsenals of both nations. Here, they are signing a treaty in December 1987 to eliminate their countries' intermediate-range nuclear missiles.

why both the United States and the Soviet Union signed the treaty, which restricted each of them to two ABM sites.

START I and II

From 1982, the United States and Soviet Union engaged in a further round of negotiations to reduce their strategic nuclear arsenals. START I (Strategic Arms Reduction Treaty) was signed in 1991, but the collapse of the Soviet Union five months later delayed it being carried out. It was finally implemented (put into force) in 2001, resulting in the destruction of about 80 per cent of all strategic nuclear weapons then in existence. A second arms reduction treaty, START II, was signed by the United States and Russia in 1993, but was never implemented.

By the mid-1990s, the arsenals of the two major nuclear powers had become less of an issue. World leaders turned their attention to the spread of nuclear weapons to other nations.

DEBATE

You are in charge

You are a diplomat from a country that is attempting to develop nuclear weapons. Your nation's main enemy already has them. You meet with representatives of the international community who want you to end your nuclear programme. How do you defend your government's decision?

- Your country needs nuclear weapons if it is to have any chance in a conflict with its nuclear-armed enemy.

- Countries that have nuclear weapons have no right to tell other nations that they cannot develop them.

- Having nuclear weapons will prevent war. Your country and its enemy would not dare go to war when both might be destroyed in a nuclear exchange.

CHAPTER 3

Tackling Nuclear Proliferation

It is 2025. Ariel lives in Tel Aviv, the second largest city in Israel. Because it is a small state surrounded by hostile neighbours, Israel has long been prepared against attacks. When Ariel is older, he will have to serve in Israel's army. But Ariel's immediate future is threatened. Israel has had its own nuclear weapons for many years. But now a nearby state, committed to the destruction of Israel, has become a fully fledged nuclear power. Israel would probably be able to retaliate against a nuclear attack with a devastating second strike. But feelings in the region are so strong that Ariel is not sure that the prospect of retaliation will be enough to deter a nuclear attack. He thinks that Israel may even use its nuclear bombs first to destroy the enemy weapons before they can be used. Ariel is angry that the international community did not do more to prevent Israel's neighbour from acquiring nuclear weapons.

The Nuclear Non-Proliferation Treaty

During the late 1960s, the international community began to recognize that the world would be safer if no more countries acquired nuclear weapons. The more nuclear weapons spread around the globe, the greater the risk of their accidental or deliberate use. This concern led to the creation of a Nuclear Non-Proliferation Treaty (NPT). The treaty was opened for signature in July 1968 and came into force in March 1970.

Non-nuclear-armed signatories pledged not to develop nuclear weapons. However, they were allowed to harness nuclear energy for peaceful purposes. As part of the treaty, nations with nuclear technology promised to help others to learn to build nuclear power stations to provide electricity. The five nuclear-armed states – the United States, the Soviet Union, Britain, France and China – agreed

not to help other nations develop nuclear weapons. The treaty was backed by inspections, carried out by the International Atomic Energy Agency (IAEA). The agency was to have access to the civilian nuclear power programmes of all non-nuclear NPT signatories and would check that illegal weapons were not being developed. By the 2000s, 189 nations had signed the treaty.

Inspectors from the International Atomic Energy Agency look over an Iranian uranium production facility. Iran allowed the 2007 visit in an effort to convince the world that it was not developing nuclear weapons.

THE INTERNATIONAL ATOMIC ENERGY AGENCY

The International Atomic Energy Agency (IAEA) is an international organization linked with the United Nations. It was set up in 1957 to promote peaceful uses of nuclear technology. It advises countries on safety procedures, helping them to use the technology without endangering their populations. The IAEA also has special 'safeguards agreements' with more than 145 states around the world. The agency inspects the civilian nuclear programmes of states that have signed the NPT and do not have nuclear weapons. In this way the IAEA can check that nuclear material is not being used to manufacture weapons. In 2005, the agency and its director general, Mohamed ElBaradei, were awarded the Nobel Peace Prize.

Proliferation in the NPT era

The NPT came into force in 1970, but its existence has not prevented the proliferation of nuclear weapons. India, Israel and Pakistan refused to sign the treaty and developed their own weapons programmes. Israel has never admitted to possessing nuclear weapons, but experts believe it developed them some time in the 1960s. As far as is known, Israel has not tested its weapons.

Successful nuclear tests were carried out by India in 1974 and by Pakistan in 1998. The fact that India and Pakistan both possess nuclear weapons is of particular concern because these two countries have fought each other on several occasions and relations between them remain fragile. This example demonstrates a way in which nuclear weapons can spread, with first one and then the other of two rival powers seeking security or advantage by acquiring 'the Bomb'.

The nuclear-armed members of the NPT, including the United States and Russia, have not helped the situation by failing to live up to their obligations under the treaty. While criticizing any state that wishes to develop nuclear weapons, they have continued to develop their own ever more powerful weapons systems. This has certainly weakened their case and damaged the cause of non-proliferation.

The end of the Cold War

In 1991, the Soviet Union collapsed and broke up into a number of independent states. The Cold War ended. The superpower

Lift off. Pakistan tests a medium-range Ghauri missile carrying a nuclear warhead. With a range of up to 1,500 kilometers, these missiles can strike at major targets within Pakistan's neighbour and enemy, India.

rivalry had been, until this time, the driving force behind the build-up of nuclear weapons. Therefore many people thought that disarmament would rapidly follow. However, the world's arsenals did not disappear. Russia, the dominant state from the former Soviet Union, was determined to maintain its status as a major nuclear power. Moreover, weapons remained stationed in the newly independent former Soviet republics, Belarus, Kazakhstan and Ukraine.

Meanwhile, new threats emerged in other parts of the world. States, including Iraq and Iran, became ambitious to acquire nuclear weapons. At the same time, Islamist terrorism became a global menace. Many people feared that dictators or terrorists might obtain the materials needed to manufacture nuclear weapons. The Cold War era, with its 'balance of terror', gave way to a different, in some ways more insecure, world.

DEBATE

You are in charge

You belong to a group that is opposed to nuclear weapons and hopes one day to see them all dismantled. Your group is divided over the issue of nuclear power. Some members want to see nuclear power stations shut down, while others only want nuclear weapons outlawed. Which side will you join, and how will you justify your choice?

- You think that your group should campaign against nuclear power as well as nuclear weapons. You argue that nuclear power production can be used as a first step to producing weapons technology.

- You think that your group should stick to its mission of opposing nuclear weapons. You believe that nuclear power may be necessary to serve the energy needs of the future as fossil fuels become scarce.

CHAPTER 4

The Nuclear Black Market

It is 2025. A nuclear weapon has been stolen from the facility where Petri works as a security guard. His country possesses a large number of nuclear weapons. But times are hard, and the economy is in crisis. Political leaders are more concerned with maintaining the supply of basic goods than with safeguarding the nuclear arsenal. The storage facility is very large, and only a few guards patrol it at any one time. There is no high-tech equipment to protect the nuclear weapons, just fences, barbed wire and padlocks. Moreover, Petri and his colleagues have not been paid for several weeks. He suspects another guard may have helped the robbers. Petri dreads to think what sort of people would want to steal a nuclear missile, and what they might use it for.

In the modern world, the information required to build a nuclear weapon is readily available in books and on the internet. A group attempting to do so would not need to establish a huge undertaking like the Manhattan Project (see pages 7–8). In 1977, an undergraduate physicist at Princeton University set out to design a plutonium bomb as his thesis project, and within five months he had successfully done so. All of the necessary information was easy to find. Today, with the help of the internet, it would be simple for someone with the right kind of scientific background to design a working bomb.

The real difficulty is not the technical know-how but getting hold of the right kind of fuel. Nuclear fuel, known as fissile material, must be very pure in order to be capable of producing a nuclear explosion. Fissile material that is pure enough to use in a bomb is referred to as weapons-grade uranium or plutonium. Nuclear power stations do not need this kind of fissile material in order to produce electricity for peaceful purposes. There is therefore little reason for a country to seek such material, unless it is trying to manufacture a nuclear weapon.

(opposite) The final stage of uranium enrichment produces a solid mass of uranium-235 like the one shown here. The metal disc in the picture weighs around four and a half kilograms and is suitable for use in a nuclear weapon.

FISSILE MATERIAL

Fissile material is needed to power a nuclear explosion. Elaborate processes are used to produce the two fissile materials used in nuclear weapons, uranium-235 and plutonium-239. Uranium-235 makes up only 1 per cent of natural uranium deposits. It has to be separated from the more common form, uranium-238, using a process called enrichment. The finished product, called highly enriched uranium (HEU), contains at least 20 per cent uranium-235. Plutonium-239 does not exist naturally. It is produced in nuclear power plants, which have reactors fuelled with uranium-238. During the reactor's operation, the uranium-238 absorbs an extra particle called a neutron and becomes plutonium-239.

At a 1999 hearing of the House Armed Services Committee on Capitol Hill, Washington DC, military adviser Peter Pry shows what a 'suitcase' nuclear weapon might look like.

Fortunately, weapons-grade material is hard to come by. It does not occur in nature and can only be produced via a complex process. Special facilities are needed for turning uranium mined from the earth into highly enriched uranium (HEU), suitable for weapons, or for reprocessing used reactor fuel into weapons-grade plutonium (see panel on page 23). These facilities are prominent and visible structures. Their presence in a country that is not supposed to be producing fissile material will immediately make IAEA inspectors suspicious.

Buying or stealing nuclear material

Because nuclear know-how is not hard to obtain, it is vital that weapons-grade fuel should not fall into the wrong hands. Without fissile material, or any way to produce it, it is impossible to build a nuclear weapon. With the fissile material, it is frighteningly easy. A rogue government or terrorist group could obtain the material either by stealing it or by buying it on the black (illegal) market.

An even more frightening situation would arise if criminals managed to steal or buy an operational nuclear weapon. The possessor of such a weapon would require almost no expertise to carry out a nuclear attack.

Such fears have intensified since the end of the Cold War. The break-up of the Soviet Union raised concerns about the fate of that formerly powerful country's nuclear arsenal and stocks of fissile materials. Observers feared that groups within the Soviet military might sell off nuclear weapons to the highest bidder. No one could (or can now) be entirely sure that all the weapons of the Soviet era were accounted for. Up to 100 small nuclear bombs, designed to be used by spies behind enemy lines in the event of war, were rumoured to be missing. These weapons are often referred to as 'suitcase nukes' because they are small enough to fit inside a suitcase or backpack. They would be ideally suited to a terrorist or sneak attack.

RESEARCH REACTORS

During the Cold War, the United States and the Soviet Union helped many countries build research reactors (used for scientific work and research). There are now at least 130 research reactors, some containing uranium pure enough to be used in a weapon. Many reactors are in countries that are too poor to keep them secure. In 1997, criminals stole highly enriched uranium from a reactor in the African nation of Zaire (now Democratic Republic of the Congo) and sold it on the black market. Police eventually tracked down the material in Italy. The US Department of Energy is a leading player in the ongoing international effort to recover vulnerable material and to secure reactors. Specialists can modify reactors to run on low enriched uranium (LEU), which cannot be used in weapons manufacture.

To add to the problems, Soviet nuclear weapons were stationed on the territories of several of its former republics, now independent states. In the 1990s, a US initiative, the Cooperative Threat Reduction (CTR) Program, organized the return of nuclear warheads in Kazakhstan, Ukraine and Belarus to Russia. The CTR also set up a long-term programme of decommissioning (putting out of use) launch sites and other nuclear facilities in the three republics.

Measures to safeguard nuclear weapons and fissile material within Russia itself were notoriously poor. The country went through a difficult period during the 1990s, and many sensitive sites were left under-protected or even unguarded. Security personnel were commonly underpaid and under-motivated. This raised concerns that they might be tempted to sell the weapons or help people steal them in exchange for money. Inspectors of Russian sites have repeatedly criticized the minimal security precautions taken. Although the Russian government's control over its nuclear infrastructure has improved in the 2000s, some experts claim that many sites are still vulnerable.

A security guard in Uzbekistan scans a vehicle with a radiation monitor. The United States provided funding for detection equipment, hoping to reduce the threat of nuclear smuggling out of the former Soviet Union.

Smuggling nuclear material

Fissile material is an attractive target for thieves, because there are nations and terrorist groups willing to pay a great deal of money for it. Between 1993 and 2005, the IAEA recorded 220 attempts to smuggle nuclear material across national borders. The thieves have often been caught in the act or captured in another country with stolen fissile material. These are only the cases that have been discovered. A successful smuggling operation would probably not be exposed until someone noticed what had been stolen. For example, in 1997 a Russian inspection of a site in Georgia, a former Soviet state, found that a significant quantity of highly enriched uranium, weighing at least 0.9 kilogrammes, was missing. Given how infrequently some sites are inspected, such thefts might not be discovered for years.

The punishments for nuclear smuggling are often surprisingly lenient. The courts in countries where smugglers are captured frequently sentence them to only about two years in prison. Some observers argue that the anti-smuggling or arms control laws under which nuclear thieves are prosecuted are inadequate. They suggest that more severe laws are needed to deal with nuclear smugglers.

A Q Khan's nuclear network

Criminals smuggle nuclear material to make money. They sell the materials to governments that wish to develop nuclear weapons, to increase their existing arsenals or to make money by selling the material themselves. The Pakistani scientist Dr Abdul Qadeer Khan ran a particularly infamous network. It sold the technologies needed to purify fissile material into a form suitable for weapons.

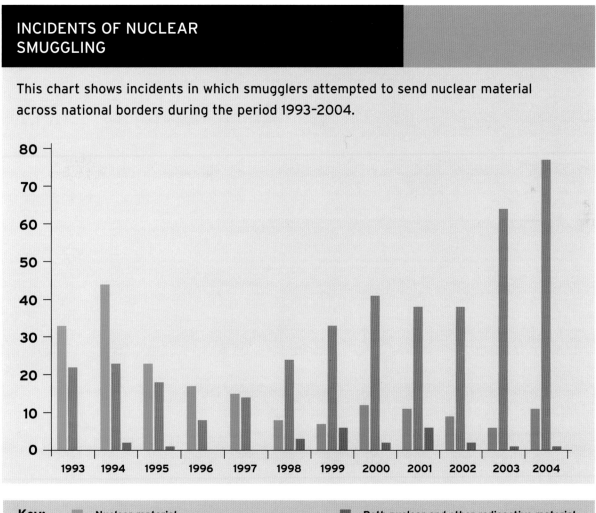

INCIDENTS OF NUCLEAR SMUGGLING

This chart shows incidents in which smugglers attempted to send nuclear material across national borders during the period 1993-2004.

Key:
- Nuclear material
- Other radioactive material
- Both nuclear and other radioactive material

Source: International Atomic Energy Agency

A Q KHAN

Dr Abdul Qadeer Khan (born 1936) is a Pakistani scientist who has been called 'the father of the Islamic bomb'. His role as the founder and mastermind of Pakistan's nuclear weapons programme made him a national hero. He subsequently became notorious for his role in the proliferation of nuclear weapons technology. In 2003, reports emerged that Pakistan had supplied components for uranium enrichment to Iran and Libya. Khan confessed that he had sold nuclear technology. He claimed he had acted without the knowledge of the Pakistani government. He has since withdrawn his confession, claiming that the government was well aware of his activities.

Though officially disgraced, A Q Khan remains a hero in the eyes of many Pakistanis as the creator of their country's nuclear weapons programme. Here, supporters flourish Khan's portrait during a 2007 march celebrating the anniversary of Pakistan's first successful nuclear test.

In 1998, under Khan's guidance, Pakistan had succeeded in testing a nuclear weapon and became the first Islamic state to join 'the nuclear club'. Initially, experts were most worried by the possibility of nuclear conflict between Pakistan and its nuclear-armed neighbour India. However, this anxiety was soon overtaken by another one. The attacks on US targets on 11 September 2001 by the Islamist terrorist network al-Qaeda provoked the fear that sympathizers within Pakistan might pass nuclear information and materials to terrorists.

The nuclear network set up by A Q Khan seems to have been motivated by profit rather than ideals. He sold components and schematics (plans showing how to make something) to customers with very different political and religious systems, such as Iran, Libya and North Korea. The IAEA described his operation as 'a Wal-Mart (a US superstore) of private sector proliferation'. His operation did not make much effort to keep its activities secret. The sales brochure Khan distributed had a picture of his own face superimposed in front of the mushroom cloud of a nuclear explosion! Some experts believe Khan's claims that the government of Pakistan was involved in his schemes.

DEBATE

You are in charge
You are an advisor working for the energy department of a developed country. Your country uses nuclear energy to generate much of its electricity. You have been asked to research nuclear smuggling. You must suggest how the government should spend its budget most efficiently to reduce this threat. What will you propose?

- Improve border policing to make sure that no radioactive material is smuggled out of your country.

- Convert research reactors to run on nuclear fuels of a type that is not suitable for use in weapons.

- Offer financial aid to foreign governments to help them guard their nuclear sites.

CHAPTER 5

Nuclear Attack

It is 2025. Elise and her family cannot leave their home. Terrorists have detonated a weapon called a 'dirty bomb' on the city's underground railway system. This kind of weapon uses explosives to spread hazardous radioactive material. The city authorities have instructed everyone to remain indoors while scientists measure the extent of the radioactive contamination. Although Elise lives far from the location of the attack, she will still be affected by it. She knows that the underground will be closed for a long time. She and thousands of others will have to find other ways of travelling around in a city where the roads are already extremely congested. This will make it harder for the city's inhabitants to work and prosper. Elise is afraid that even more damaging attacks may follow.

Nuclear weapons and their proliferation remain a very real threat to the modern world. Many experts rate the likelihood of a nuclear incident as being very high. A report by the US Senate Foreign Relations Committee in 2005 took the bleak view that there was a 29 per cent likelihood of a nuclear strike on American soil by 2015.

The present-day situation is very different from that of the Cold War. The superpower rivalry was frightening, but the two sides developed codes and rules that helped to keep the peace. After the Cuban Missile Crisis, a permanent telephone hotline, known as the 'red telephone', allowed the US president and the Soviet leader to contact each other immediately in the event of a crisis. During the 1970s, arms control negotiations ensured that talks between the two sides would go on continuously. In the modern world, there are fewer rules and enemies are harder to identify.

DIRTY BOMBS

A 'dirty bomb' is the common name for a radiological weapon. This is a conventional bomb packed with radioactive material, which scatters when the bomb goes off. Dirty bombs are not true nuclear bombs, because there is no nuclear chain reaction and therefore no enormous explosion. They are designed instead to disperse radiation over as wide an area as possible. Terrorists could make a dirty bomb using commonly found radioactive isotopes such as caesium, used in radiotherapy for cancer patients.

CURRENT NUCLEAR ARSENALS

These are the estimated world nuclear arsenals in 2008:

Country	Estimated number of nuclear weapons
China	250-320
France	350
India	50
Israel	100-200
North Korea	5-12
Pakistan	40-70
Russia	7,200
United Kingdom	180-200
United States	5,736

Source: Center for Defense Information

During the Cold War, people dreaded the possibility of a nuclear attack. In the United States, many families installed their own bomb shelters, stocked with tinned food, in which to take refuge if war broke out.

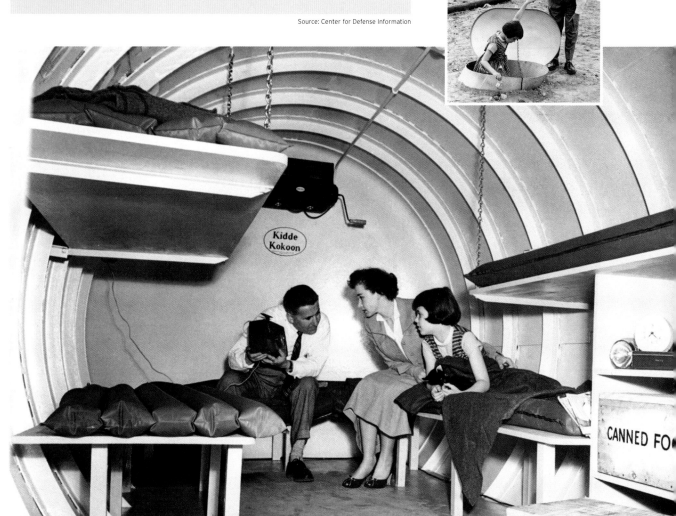

Kidde Kokoon

CANNED FO

Moreover, while the United States and the Soviet Union had very different political systems and beliefs, both were motivated by national and material interests and, on the whole, behaved rationally. Neither desired their own destruction, so the principle of MAD (see page 13) acted as a useful deterrent against aggression.

In recent times, however, with the rise of Islamist terrorism, the strategy of deterrence may no longer prove so effective. The behaviour of Islamist terrorists is neither rational nor predictable. Suicide bombers, for example, seem driven by a wish to destroy that is stronger than any concern for their own lives. That makes them extremely hard to defend against. One of the great fears of the modern world is that such people might obtain nuclear weapons.

NUCLEAR TERRORISM IN FICTION

There have been several fictional portrayals of nuclear terrorism. A well-known example was the 1991 novel *The Sum of All Fears*, by Tom Clancy, in which terrorists plan to detonate a nuclear weapon at American football's Super Bowl. In the sixth season of the Fox television drama *24*, the terrorists succeed in detonating a nuclear device in Los Angeles, California. And the 2004 BBC TV movie *A Dirty War* depicted the impact of a dirty bomb attack in London.

Disaster scenario: nuclear terrorism

For many people, the threat of nuclear weapons has taken on a new urgency since the events of 11 September 2001, often shortened to '9/11'. The 9/11 attacks were the work of the Islamist terrorist network al-Qaeda. The terrorists hijacked four planes, intending to crash them into major targets within the United States. They crashed two of the planes into the twin towers of the World Trade Center in New York City, and a third into the Pentagon in Virginia, which houses the US Department of Defense. Passengers on the fourth plane attempted to overpower the hijackers. The terrorists –

probably realizing they were going to lose control of the plane – crashed it in a field in Pennsylvania without reaching their target, the Capitol Building in Washington, DC.

The attack demonstrated what an organized terrorist group, eager to kill on a grand scale, could achieve, especially if its members were prepared to die. If fanatical terrorists like these could obtain the right materials from the black market and obtain the assistance of sympathetic scientists, the nightmare of a terrorist nuclear weapon could become a reality.

Firemen make their way through the rubble following the 9/11 attack on the World Trade Center. Many New York firefighters lost their lives through their heroic efforts to save people and contain the destruction.

Disaster scenario: nuclear war

Despite the collapse of the Soviet Union and the end of the Cold War, the United States and Russia remain prepared for a nuclear conflict with each other. Old habits die hard, and the United States continues to run war games (large-scale military rehearsals) in which Russia is the opponent in a nuclear war. On the Russian side, scientists continue to improve the country's missiles, with the aim of ensuring that Russian nuclear weapons could penetrate any US ABM system.

Nonetheless, a war between the old enemies is currently unlikely. Nuclear-tipped ballistic missiles are more likely to be used in other conflicts. China is engaged in a long-term dispute with the island of Taiwan, which it regards as a rebel province and refuses to recognize as an independent nation. In a nightmare scenario, China might use its nuclear weapons against Taiwan, prompting a nuclear response against China by the West. Any such war would involve nuclear weapons far more powerful than the bombs dropped on Japan in 1945.

Disaster scenario: concealed nuclear device

A disturbing fact about nuclear weapons is that they are extremely hard to detect. Instruments cannot easily distinguish between background radiation, which is present everywhere, and a bomb with a uranium core. The latest scanners are better than ever at identifying different types of radiation, but these have quite a short range. The danger therefore remains that devices will be smuggled across national borders undetected.

Fewer than 5 per cent of cargo containers entering the United States are opened and inspected by customs officers. Many illegal items, such as drugs, are smuggled into the United States by sea, passing through the ports in containers. Using such methods, a terrorist group or a hostile government

ATOMIC DETECTIVES

In 1974, hoaxers claimed to have placed a nuclear bomb in the US city of Boston and threatened to detonate it. In response to the incident, President Gerald Ford established Nuclear Emergency Support Teams (NEST). The NEST teams are made up of expert volunteers. They are sent with scanning equipment to investigate potential nuclear threats. They often travel in disguise, and so are sometimes known as 'nuclear ninjas'.

could smuggle a nuclear bomb into the United States or some other country in order to carry out a sneak attack.

Disaster scenario: attack on a nuclear power station

If would-be attackers could not obtain a nuclear weapon of their own, they might decide to target a nuclear power plant instead. The 1986 accident at the civilian reactor at Chernobyl in the Ukraine (then part of the Soviet Union) contaminated a wide area. A similar result could be achieved deliberately, for example by terrorists, if they managed to damage a nuclear reactor.

An explosion takes place at a mock nuclear facility in Nevada, USA, as part of a training exercise. The site is used to train emergency response personnel.

In order to spread radiation from the reactor, saboteurs would have to penetrate its containment building. This is a hefty, airtight structure designed to keep radiation inside, even in the event of a meltdown (the overheating and melting of nuclear fuel in the reactor core). Since the use of planes as offensive weapons in the 9/11 attacks, experts have discussed – and disagreed about – whether a plane, intentionally crashed into a reactor, could achieve this effect.

Another target at a power plant could be the pool of water used to cool down the spent fuel rods. The rods are highly radioactive and extremely hot. The cold water prevents them from melting and releasing their radiation into the environment. If terrorists were somehow able to drain the pool, the rods would melt and give off large quantities of harmful radiation.

Firemen in Seattle, Washington, take part in a 2003 simulation of a dirty bomb attack. They wear anti-contamination suits to protect them from radiation.

DIRTY BOMB IN MOSCOW

On 23 November 1995 a dirty bomb containing the radioisotope caesium-137 and a mixture of explosives was discovered in Ismailovsky Park in Moscow, Russia. It had been placed there by Chechen separatists, fighting for independence from Russia. The Chechens decided not to detonate the weapon but to gain publicity for their cause by telling television journalists where it was. Although no harm was done, the incident highlighted the potential danger of a terrorist attack using a dirty bomb.

After 9/11, the US Nuclear Regulatory Commission (NRC) admitted that none of the 103 reactors in the United States had been designed to withstand the impact of a jetliner. However, since the attacks, the NRC has studied the problem and worked to improve the defences of US nuclear plants. Their studies found it unlikely that a plane could cause damage serious enough to release large quantities of radiation.

Disaster scenario: dirty bomb

Experts agree that it would be extremely difficult to cause mass casualties with a dirty bomb attack. However, a dirty bomb could cause widespread panic and disruption. It could also contaminate a large area for a long time, requiring the evacuation of the population and bringing businesses and transport systems to a halt.

DEBATE

You are in charge

You are a member of the United Nations (UN) Terrorism Prevention Branch. You are in talks with the representatives of various nations, discussing the best ways to prevent a nuclear terrorist attack. The representatives are urging the development of new technologies to detect the radioactive cores of nuclear weapons. Current technologies require close-range scans to detect possible threats and cannot easily distinguish radioactive cores from background radiation. What do you say?

- You agree with their focus on new technologies. We need to be able to find and disarm nuclear weapons if they are smuggled into our cities.
- You argue that the money would be better spent on increasing security at ports and airports, particularly manual checking of baggage and freight.

CHAPTER 6

Meeting the Challenge

It is 2025. Sarah is an expert on international relations and non-proliferation. She heads a team that has been asked to work on new approaches to halting proliferation. Recent threats from rogue states and terrorist groups have forced the international community to act more aggressively. Security at nuclear installations has already been strengthened. Sarah's team has just completed a report suggesting new measures, and it has been well received by the United Nations. It recommends a system of consistent and fair penalties for states that do not comply with the international inspection regime. Sarah is optimistic that the world will soon agree on a united approach to reducing the threat of nuclear proliferation.

The Nuclear Non-Proliferation Treaty that came into force in 1970 has had its successes. The most striking of these involved South Africa. During the 1970s, South Africa developed nuclear weapons. But in 1992 it became the first state in history to give up its nuclear arsenal, signing the Non-Proliferation Treaty and allowing IAEA inspectors into the country to dismantle the existing weapons.

The Non-Proliferation Treaty has also made it more difficult for other nations to develop nuclear weapons. Treaty members are forbidden to export materials and technology for nuclear weapons, forcing aspiring nuclear states to turn to the black market. IAEA inspectors, provided they can get access, can detect nuclear weapons programmes before they are completed.

Despite this, the Non-Proliferation Treaty's success has been limited. The current nuclear club members show no sign of giving up their weapons, and South Africa remains a unique case of voluntary disarmament. Most significantly, there are now more nuclear-armed

A Ukrainian officer surveys a decommissioned missile silo on 30 October 2001. On this date, Ukraine destroyed the last of its ICBM silos as part of a US-funded plan to make it into a non-nuclear-armed state.

states than there were in 1970. Information on how to construct nuclear bombs is readily available. Some of the vital fissile material that could be used to construct a weapon is not well guarded. Some completed weapons built during the Cold War may be stored insecurely, or may have disappeared, perhaps finding their way into the possession of dangerous organizations or regimes. Consequently, the international community is faced with difficult challenges.

Securing fissile material

Keeping fissile material out of the wrong hands requires a determined effort. The Cooperative Threat Reduction Program (CTR) is an important initiative in this direction. The CTR was set up in 1991, thanks to the efforts of two US senators, Sam Nunn and Richard Lugar, to help dismantle weapons in the former Soviet Union. The CTR project continues to help dispose of old weapons, dismantling sites and securing nuclear materials. Its supporters believe it should receive more funding, but its opponents argue that the money would be better spent in strengthening US defences.

The chart shows US federal (central government) funding for the Cooperative Threat Reduction Program.

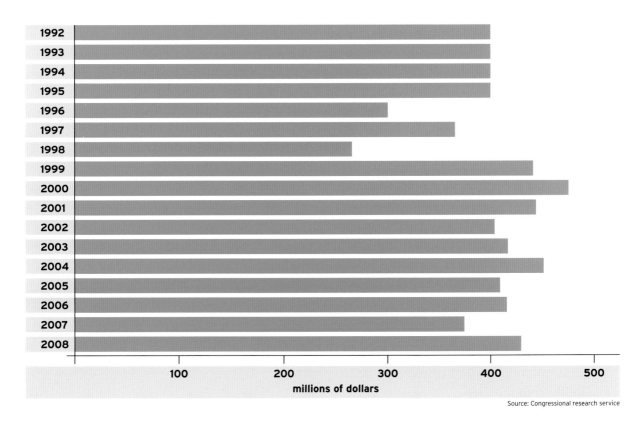

Source: Congressional research service

Many experts, including Sam Nunn and Mohamed ElBaradei, director general of the IAEA, have called for a system of greater international oversight of fissile material production. They believe that the international community as a whole should monitor the production of nuclear fuel. This would allow greater openness and scrutiny. It would also reduce the opportunities for black market operations and make it harder to produce weapons-grade materials secretly.

Non-proliferation diplomacy: Iran

The Middle Eastern state of Iran is at the centre of a current proliferation crisis. In 2006 Iran succeeded in enriching uranium. Uranium enrichment was not in itself a breach of the Non-Proliferation Treaty. However, many in the international community feared that Iran might go on to develop a nuclear weapons programme. Iran insists that it does not want to develop nuclear weapons, only nuclear power. The possibility of an Iranian nuclear bomb is particularly worrying for the United States and other Western countries. Iran is ruled by an Islamist regime that has been very hostile to the West and Israel. Iran also has ties with Islamist terrorists.

Iran has insisted on continuing to enrich uranium, despite a United Nations (UN) Security Council resolution ordering it to stop. The UN has imposed economic sanctions (restrictions on trade) on Iran, but these have not persuaded it to stop its programme. Negotiators have offered Iran incentives to agree, such as help in modernizing the country's industries. In June 2008, the five permanent members of the UN Security Council (the United States, the United Kingdom, Russia, France and China) offered to help Iran build two nuclear reactors and guaranteed a regular supply of nuclear fuel. Iran, however, remained defiant.

SHUTTING DOWN THE BLACK MARKET

The nuclear black market poses a serious threat, but determined action can bring positive results. In 2003, the United States stopped an illegal shipment of nuclear components heading for Libya, a North African state with a record of sympathy for terrorism. The components were needed for the uranium enrichment process. They had been supplied by the nuclear network of Pakistan's 'rocket man' A Q Khan (see pages 27-29). Caught red-handed, Libya admitted having a secret nuclear weapons programme, in violation of the Non-Proliferation Treaty, and promised to disband it.

Counter-proliferation diplomacy: North Korea

The most recent addition to the nuclear club, North Korea, successfully performed a nuclear test in 2006. North Korea is ruled by an erratic and unpredictable dictator, which makes its possession of nuclear weapons particularly worrying. North Korea's missiles lack the range to threaten the United States mainland, but they pose a direct threat to North Korea's neighbours in East Asia, including South Korea (with whom it has waged war in the past) and Japan.

In 2003 a South Korean protester burns the North Korean flag next to a model of a nuclear missile. North Korea's nuclear programme caused fear and outrage in South Korea.

The international community has made strong diplomatic efforts to persuade North Korea to dismantle its nuclear weapons programme. Hopes for a solution rest on the long-running Six-Party Talks involving North Korea, China, South Korea, the United States, Russia and Japan.

There is no immediate prospect of the North Koreans giving up their weapons. However, negotiations have made some progress towards halting the country's production of additional nuclear material. In October 2008, North Korea agreed to US demands to halt plutonium production and allow inspectors to visit its nuclear sites. In return, the US State Department removed North Korea from its list of state sponsors of terrorism. Some critics feel that the agreement is inadequate, because North Korea may have secret nuclear sites. North Korea suffers from regular shortages of food and electricity, and may eventually be persuaded to give up its nuclear weapons in exchange for foreign aid and an end to sanctions.

The military option

When politicians lose patience with diplomacy, they often turn to military action. Since US President George W Bush declared a 'war on terror', following the 9/11 attacks, the United States and its allies have engaged in a number of military operations. In the immediate aftermath of 9/11, a US-led coalition invaded Afghanistan, where the ruling Taliban were sheltering al-Qaeda terrorists. When intelligence agents explored deserted al-Qaeda camps in Afghanistan, they found evidence of the terrorists' interest in nuclear technology, including bomb schematics. This discovery reinforced Western fears of a terrorist organization linking up with a rogue state to acquire and master nuclear technology.

In 2003, the United States and its allies undertook another military intervention. They toppled the Iraqi dictator Saddam Hussein, who was suspected of trying to develop nuclear or other weapons of mass destruction. It turned out that Hussein had not been able to develop such programmes and the war was widely criticized. However, many governments continue to view the military option as a necessary last resort in cases where nuclear proliferation poses a direct threat to world peace and security.

(opposite) This satellite photograph shows a site in Syria that was bombed by Israeli planes in 2007. The Israelis claimed that it was a nuclear facility, part of a secret Syrian nuclear weapons programme, though Syria denied the charge. Israel is determined to prevent its hostile Arab neighbours from obtaining 'the Bomb'.

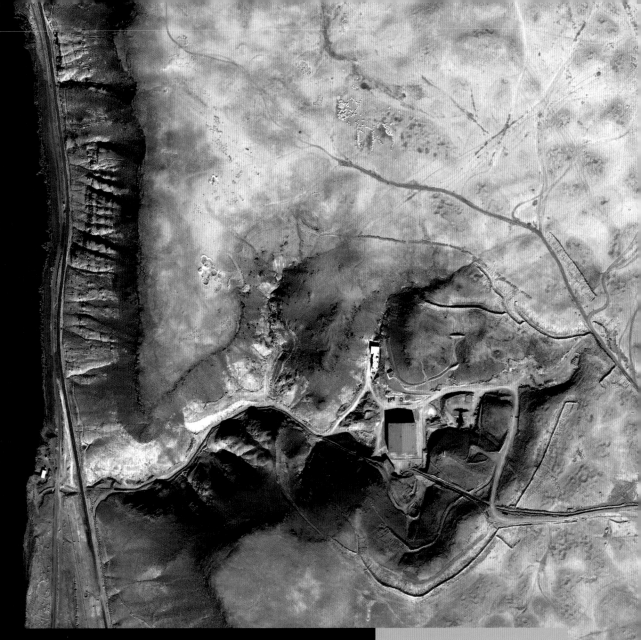

ISRAEL'S COUNTER-PROLIFERATION STRIKES

Israel is a small Jewish state in the Middle East. It is friendly with the West and is surrounded by hostile Arab neighbours. Israel has nuclear weapons of its own and has been aggressive in its efforts to prevent neighbouring Arab regimes from acquiring them. Israel's actions may have helped to prevent nuclear proliferation, although its motive was simply self-defence.

■ On 7 June 1981, Israel carried out an air strike against an Iraqi nuclear reactor. The Israelis claimed that Iraq planned to use the reactor to produce nuclear weapons, which could be used against Israel.

■ On 6 September 2007, Israel bombed a site in Syria. The Israelis claimed that the site held a reactor capable of producing plutonium-239 for nuclear weapons.

THE COMPREHENSIVE TEST BAN TREATY

In 1996, a new international treaty, the Comprehensive Test Ban Treaty (CTBT), was proposed. The treaty banned all nuclear tests, improving on the Partial Test Ban Treaty of 1963, which permitted underground tests (see page 15). By 2008, the CTBT had been signed by 180 states. However, the treaty is still not in force. It cannot become operational until certain key, nuclear-armed countries have ratified (formally approved) it, and not all of them are yet willing to do so. The countries who have not ratified the treaty include Pakistan, India, North Korea and the United States.

Survivors of the nuclear strike on Hiroshima remember the victims of the attack. They are burning incense and offering prayers at the Peace Memorial Park in Hiroshima, Japan, in 2008, on the 63rd anniversary of the event.

Moving towards disarmament

For as long as nuclear weapons have existed there have been calls for them to be abolished. In the modern world, with its nine nuclear-armed states, the goal of total disarmament seems further away than ever. Nuclear-armed states are unwilling to give up their weapons while others still have them. They also enjoy the power and status that goes with membership of the nuclear club.

A world free of nuclear weapons may become a reality one day, but the immediate task is to stop their proliferation. Reducing stockpiles of weapons would be an important first step, limiting the danger of an accidental nuclear launch or detonation. The global community must be ready to help countries that have difficulties securing their fissile material. All nations will have to be careful to prevent unauthorized nuclear traffic across their borders.

Regular inspection and improved technology should ensure that states cannot produce the material they need to develop nuclear bombs. Internationally agreed and enforced penalties would help to deter both would-be suppliers of nuclear materials and countries tempted to try and develop nuclear weapons. A consistent approach, backed by the entire international community, seems the only hope of tackling and reversing proliferation.

By shrinking their own arsenals, the nuclear-armed states could set an example to the rest of the world. If countries that have nuclear weapons refuse to give them up, convincing other countries not to develop them remains an uphill battle. Everyone fears a nuclear attack, and as long as having nuclear weapons is seen as a deterrent to nuclear attack, other nations will continue to want to develop them in self-defence. Nuclear proliferation poses a grave threat to the future of the world. If we do nothing, there may not be a future.

DEBATE

You are in charge

You are a delegate to the United Nations. Reliable intelligence suggests that an aggressive power is attempting to build a nuclear weapon. Member states cannot agree about what should be done. Some favour a military invasion to remove the aggressive regime from power, while others prefer to impose economic sanctions until IAEA inspectors are allowed into the country. Which approach will you advocate?

■ Economic sanctions, because an invasion is likely to be costly in lives and resources.

■ Invasion, based on the argument that economic sanctions work very slowly and sometimes not at all. The aggressive power must not be given time to complete its nuclear programme.

Glossary

al-Qaeda An Islamist terrorist network led by the Saudi Arabian, Osama bin Laden. It was responsible for the 9/11 attacks.

atom The smallest unit of matter that is identifiable as a specific chemical element.

black market An illegal market where stolen or illicit items are bought and sold.

blockade An action that prevents supplies from reaching a country.

Cold War The worldwide struggle for power and influence between the United States and the Soviet Union, together with their respective allies, which lasted from 1945 to 1990.

communism A system, or the belief in a system, in which capitalism is overthrown and the state controls wealth and property.

deterrence A strategy of discouraging enemy attack by maintaining sufficient military force to retaliate.

fallout Radioactive contamination left behind by a nuclear explosion.

fissile material Radioactive material suitable for creating a nuclear reaction.

highly enriched uranium (HEU) Uranium that has been processed to make it suitable for use in weapons.

intercontinental ballistic missile (ICBM) A long-range missile used to attack distant countries. An ICBM can be fitted with a nuclear warhead.

isotope A form of an element that differs from other forms of the same element because it has a different number of neutrons. Only specific isotopes can be used as nuclear fuel.

monopoly Complete control or ownership by a single individual, organization or country.

mushroom cloud The cloud of condensed gas and debris produced by a very powerful explosion. The mushroom cloud has become a symbol of nuclear war and destruction.

Nazi regime The government of Adolf Hitler's National Socialist Party, which ruled Germany from 1933 to 1945.

nuclear fission The process of splitting the nucleus of an atom to release energy.

nuclear fusion The process in which the nuclei of light atoms, such as hydrogen and deuterium, combine to form a heavier nucleus, releasing energy.

nucleus The cluster of particles at the centre of an atom.

plutonium A metallic element used in the production of nuclear weapons.

radiation Energy emitted in the form of particles by substances such as uranium and plutonium, whose atoms are not stable and are spontaneously decaying.

republic A state with a system of government in which supreme power is in the hands of representatives elected by the people.

rogue state A term sometimes used to describe states ruled by erratic dictatorial regimes, many of which oppress their own people and sponsor terrorism.

sanctions Economic measures intended to punish a state or make it change its policies. For example, another country or an international organization may cease trading with the target state.

smuggling Illegally bringing something across a national border.

Soviet Union Also known as the USSR (Union of Soviet Socialist Republics), a country consisting of Russia and a number of other East European, Baltic and Central Asian states. The leading communist power, the Soviet Union existed from 1922 to 1991.

superpower A term used during the Cold War to describe the United States and the Soviet Union. Today, the USA is regarded as the sole superpower.

United Nations An international organization, created in 1945 to foster cooperation and friendship between nations.

uranium A metallic element used in the manufacture of nuclear weapons.

weapons of mass destruction (WMD) Weapons that are designed to kill and destroy on a very large scale. The main WMDs are nuclear, chemical and biological weapons.

Further Information

Books

Global Organizations: The International Atomic Energy Agency by Russell B Olwell (Chelsea House Publishers, 2008)

Impact: Nuclear Proliferation: The Problems and Possibilities by Glen A Cheney (Franklin Watts, 1999)

In the News: Nukes: The Spread of Nuclear Weapons by Steve Minneus (Rosen Publishing Group, 2007)

Issues in Focus Today: Weapons of Mass Destruction: The Threat of Chemical, Biological and Nuclear Weapons by Tracey A Phillips (Enslow, 2007)

Witness to History: Hiroshima by Nathaniel Harris (Heinemann, 2004)

Websites

www.nrc.gov/reading-rm/basic-ref/students.html
The US Nuclear Regulatory Commission's introduction to nuclear power, reactors, radiation, disaster prevention and more.

www.eyewitnesstohistory.com/hiroshima.htm
This site contains eyewitness accounts of key moments in history. This page describes the bombing of Hiroshima.

library.thinkquest.org/17940/texts/fission/fission.html
An animated explanation of a nuclear fission chain reaction.

www.nuclearterrorism.org/faq.html
Answers to frequently asked questions about the possibility of nuclear terrorism. Elsewhere on the site is an application called 'Blast Maps', which can visualize the frightening consequences a nuclear strike would have on a location of your choice.

www.nuclearfiles.org/
Very detailed information about nuclear weapons, energy and issues for those who want to explore further.

Debate Panel Answers

Page 9:
A strong case can be made against a country keeping its nuclear weapons. Many believe that their destructive power is so great that they should never be used in any circumstances. Organizations like the Campaign for Nuclear Disarmament (CND) in Britain urge the government to give up its nuclear weapons regardless of what anyone else does. They argue that somebody must take the lead or, sooner or later, an accident or conflict will trigger a nuclear war. On the other hand, a nation that sheds its weapons leaves itself vulnerable to attack by nuclear-armed powers. It may find itself threatened, bullied or even invaded by an aggressive regime. Should a country take the lead in disarming, or could progress be made through small, simultaneous reductions on all sides? There are no 'right' answers to questions such as these.

Page 17:
Other nations will understandably fear that your country's acquisition of nuclear weapons will add to the tensions in the region. It would probably be better not to argue about the possibility of a nuclear war. Other nations will be concerned about the damage inflicted on both sides, but they will also worry about the effects of radioactive fallout on the environment globally and within their own territories. It might be better to argue that the possession of nuclear weapons by both sides is more likely to preserve the peace. This, after all, is the basis of deterrence, which many believe prevented a war between the United States and the Soviet Union during the Cold War. Neither argument is likely to win over the international community, whose main objective is to halt nuclear proliferation.

Page 21:
Legitimate arguments can certainly be made against nuclear power - for example, radioactive nuclear waste is very difficult to dispose of. However, the fact that a country develops nuclear energy does not necessarily mean it will be able to go on from there to create nuclear weapons. An effective IAEA inspection programme coupled with a coordinated international system of penalties should be able to prevent this from happening.

Page 29:
Fissile materials are essential to the manufacture of nuclear weapons, so it is vital to store such materials securely. Strengthening checks at international borders will certainly improve success rates against smuggling. Yet however diligent the checks, it will never be possible to catch every smuggler. For this reason, preventing them from getting the fissile material in the first place should be the top priority. Greater international cooperation would be very helpful in the fight against nuclear smuggling. A united effort could be made to secure and track fissile materials, and all nations could agree to impose tough penalties on nuclear smugglers.

Page 37:
New technologies would be a great asset in improving the detection of nuclear weapons. However, they take time to develop, and the threat of nuclear terrorism is imminent. At present an unknown amount of fissile material is unaccounted for. Even more seriously, complete nuclear weapons from the former Soviet Union may have gone missing. No one can be certain if and when terrorists might get their hands on a nuclear weapon. Therefore the priority should be to increase border security. Of course, countries that can afford it should also invest in the development of more sensitive scanning devices.

Page 45:
Diplomatic and economic pressure is always preferable to military action. However, many would argue that military action is sometimes necessary when dealing with a very aggressive, unreasonable or unstable regime. If such a regime looks likely to acquire nuclear weapons, the international community must then debate the pros and cons of military action. Much will depend on intelligence estimates of how close the regime is to completing its weapons programme. If the weapons are almost ready, a swift military strike against suspected weapons sites may be the safest action. But can intelligence estimates be trusted? When deciding how to act, one should also consider the record of the regime: has it repeatedly tried to develop nuclear or other weapons of mass destruction? If the weapons programme is not advanced, it may be best to apply diplomatic pressure followed by a programme of economic sanctions and, maybe, offers of economic aid.

Index

Page numbers in **bold** refer to illustrations and charts.